GRACE YEE

JOSS: A HISTORY

NEW POEMS

First published 2025
from the Writing and Society Research Centre
at Western Sydney University
by the Giramondo Publishing Company
PO Box 557
Willoughby NSW 2068 Australia
www.giramondopublishing.com

Cover and design by Jenny Grigg
Typesetting by Andrew Davies
in 9/15 pt Tiempos Regular

Printed and bound by Pegasus Media & Logistics
Distributed in Australia by NewSouth Books

A catalogue record for this
book is available from the
National Library of Australia.

ISBN: 978-1-923106-31-4

The Giramondo Publishing Company acknowledges the support
of Western Sydney University in the implementation of its book
publishing program.

This project has been assisted by the Commonwealth Government
through Creative Australia, its arts funding and advisory body.

***Joss: A History* follows Grace Yee's debut collection *Chinese Fish*, which was awarded the Victorian Prize for Literature, the Victorian Premier's Literary Award for Poetry and the Ockham New Zealand Book Award for Poetry.**

In the White Hills Cemetery in Bendigo the remains of more than a thousand 'chinamen' lie interred, many in unmarked graves. Most were sojourners, who hailed from the Canton region in south China, and found themselves unable to return to their homeland. *Joss: A History* is inspired by the lived experiences of these early settlers, and their compatriots and descendants across Victoria and New South Wales, and Aotearoa New Zealand. The poems pay tribute to the author's ancestors, illuminating how they survived – and thrived – amid longstanding colonialist stories that have exoticised and diminished Chinese communities in white settler nations around the Pacific Rim since the gold rushes of the nineteenth century. Refracted through a twenty-first century lens, *Joss* is grounded in the conviction that the past is not past, that historical events reverberate insistently in the present.

Part poetry, part prose poetry, part found poetry, part story and history, or part social commentary, this is a short collection of timepieces...designed to capture a cacophony of lost voices, scattered over a sea of Chinese cemeteries, and symbolized by a single self-acclamation: 'I'm a can't'. Ouyang Yu

Yee is a poet of conviction, a thought-provoking and distinctive voice in Australasian literature. Alison Wong

Also by Grace Yee

Chinese Fish

for my father, whose wonder lit the world for me

Contents

Moon sitting
In one of the world's largest coal mines

longest imperial dragon

in the heritage reading room the eyes are dry, and the throat.
there are many right brain fatalities, illness from scurvy, a ten-
pound landing tax. without fail, they give multiple versions of

'no': 'ask your father' 'don't bet on it' 'wait and try again'.
sun loong 新龍, the world's longest imperial dragon, poses
a major architectural challenge. he is over one hundred metres

long, his head weighs twenty-nine kilograms and he needs
to leave the museum at easter. the doctor at the superclinic
listens to the suppuration – a grieving – in my lungs. eat the

right foods, discard evil spirits, lie low on the floor, remember:
life is good *because arable land was scarce* in sun ning 新寧
and your fathers walked three hundred and twenty-three

miles without female companionship from robe to the bendigo
goldfields. in 1857, *205464 ounces of gold were shipped*
to canton china from the victorian goldfields *at various levels*

of seaworthiness. twenty-five years later, the community
imported one hundred wooden cases of processional regalia,
designed with chinese symbolism in mind. highest quality,

bright and colourful. the sartorial epitome was a well-made
silk jacket *embroidered with four-clawed dragons surrounded*
by red and blue cirrus clouds. even the supposedly

androgynous gun yum 觀音 would agree that we need wiles
to survive. but women's clothing tends to be flimsy and poorly
made and chain stitch, while more textured, has a sturdier

effect on the lines trailing up our skirts. bookman old style
is too sedate for this poem, sans serifs more appropriate
for dismantling. one of my students is passionate about russian

formalism and defamiliarisation: a most promising frame
for white chrysanthemums and burning paper boats and houses,
for on this altar, all gods are alienated. they excluded

yeh yeh 爺爺 from the army because he had the *horns*
of a deer, the *eyes of a rabbit*, and *non-european ancestry*.
additionally, his spleen was too vigorous. listen to your

migraines, your burning hands – they are shutting down
our subjectivities. numerologically speaking, 2020 is a 9-year,
a year of incurable endings. the fortune-teller said, watch

out for a man with two heads more interested in the snapshot
of your smashed-up car and the blood on your face than your
lingering epistaxis. paw paw 婆婆 said, the way through

the immigration restriction act is through the prime minister's
stomach. after *the second world war chinese restaurants*
became gwei lo 鬼佬 palatable. when I landed, the offices

were still monotone. in 1887 the exotica of sandhurst town
– its *tea importers, herbalists, three opium dealers* – burned
to the ground. in the aftermath, our people developed

dysphasia and difficulties breathing, but the town looked
felicitously like some of the pages had been copied and
scanned and cut to fit their particular dialect. sun loong 新龍

is a strict vegetarian. they feed him pomelo leaves. his body
*is covered with six thousand silk scales, each decorated with
twenty-three tiny hand-cut mirrors*, and his eyes are dotted

with blood wrung from chickens. who will save us when
the oceans are burning and we can no longer sail home?
we are all the time treading water and nursing our amnesias,

waving flags – not white like surrender, funerals, and zirconia
dental crowns, but red like sun niang 新娘, mun yuet 滿月
and april 15, 1983: sun loong 新龍 bowing *nine times to*

prince charles and princess diana looking down from the *balcony
of the shamrock hotel* in bendigo. auspicious ancestral meanings
– *highest quality, bright and colourful*. in the presence of royalty,

the universe clears like cloud and wind and camphor.

the march

Erasing *The Bulletin: Anti-Chinaman Special Number* 14 April 1888:

mater ground[s] the sources of production what

feverous haste

this monkey gulps

tomorrow

[ ] must

infest settle and

cut-throat

all history light

conquer plains

frontier

ancient forests

feed

West-profaned

sanctuaries

wound the body of the nation

arouse

the charts of empire

here is gold

angularity

a crucible

the work

Erasing *The Bulletin: Anti-Chinaman Special Number* 14 April 1888:

lately, draymen
feeders, miners encroach without

amiability

degenerate

black river

mountains command simple story of

fair claim faithfully

Australian character
prevail[s]

the model ancestry

foreigners

surrender to

everlasting

white planet history

zealous
plunder

premises

unpardonable space
fever

British chattels
charm

far at sea

chinoiserie

at the 19th-century frontier, the WESTERN MUSEUM OF ART acquired chinese jade bronze porcelain to the value of [ ] pounds sterling: spiritual depths in a peach-bloom vase shipped without receipts. the china europeans covet: a new worldview, catalogued and deciphered, confucian curiosities bought for half a crown. the far east is a vital artery, but it does not occur to them to check the eyes for signs of life.   in the late 13th century marco polo returned to venice after seventeen years in china. he had the kit but he didn't know the incantations.   before the outbreak of world war one, ezra pound discovered chinese petals on a wet black bough in paris.   human closeness is a fragile tree, its foliage must be carefully tended. shoulder to shoulder they grow rice, build their own houses, engraft their most ancient ontological notions, their pulp continually agitated, laid out to dry in windows for all the world to see: checkout operators working around the clock, long queues of unspeakable insomnia, numberless green ordeals chafing furiously.   the world's first essay was printed from stone blocks, the squares' black characters pressed in white. like the windows of their houses facing an inner courtyard, their pages are folded on the outer edges of books, leaves uncut: protection against catastrophes, the usual classifications: animals that are eaten, and those that are not.

slides

they are imperturbable people, virulent vectors without nerves

when gold sloped we became merchantminerstorekeeper
at the bottom of the ocean where the crust is thinnest

their method of containment, deep holes quietly dug

inside we were volcanoes, phoenix in the sky,
iron flailings in magnetic reversals

their vapours are unknowable

corresponding to the western calendar we spied floaters
a hundred years to the east

in their natural habitat, their secrets are wired
in peculiar blood-humouring enclosures

they fossilised our stories on a solitary brick burner:
O R I E N T A L S: slumbered under saddlers' ash

their traditional remedies are a common resort for 21st-century pain:
real or imagined griefs, closed-track anxieties
(the amygdala, the calm)

colonial imperial indolence beneath a single moon,
the same loose stones

Playful Bodily Harm

Outbreak of Larrikinism at the Chinese Quarter. At seven o'clock in the evening, Ah Ken/Ah Long/Ah Chu was seen running up from the direction of Albert-street, calling out 'Murder!' 'Larrikins!' A well-dressed Chinaman named Sing Hop Sing/Chu Man Chu/Wing Wong Wu had been shanghaied to the ground as he got off the 'bus. Drunk and Disorderly Defendants Deny Involvement. Witness said they were home in bed all evening. Defendants Deny 'Shanghai'. Witness said they used slingshots. Four Young Larrikins in Laundry Attack. Brutal Assault on Chinaman Sam Lee/Ah Hin/Yee Moon in Victoria-parade, Fitzroy. Wounded by brick/jemmy/piece of road metal smote over left eye/back of head/thigh. Assailants Absconded, Unknown and Gregarious on the corner of Queensberry-street and Lygon-street. Constable said, 'It is a great shame there was blood flowing from the Chinaman's head.' His Honor said, 'I regret I have no power to order the lash.' Doctor said, 'I am afraid the eye will be permanently useless.' No oculist has been consulted. Ten witnesses saw Playful Bodily Harm inflicted on Ah Hing/Chew Sing/An Yong Saturday night in Market-lane. Twenty-six-year-old bricklayer's laborer from Carlton knocked Ah Hing/Chew Sing/An Yong to the ground. Kicked him savagely about the body. Jumped on the victim's chest until he expired. The Chinaman's compatriot reported that after the Larrikin had done the Mischief 'he walk away no concern'. Chinese cabinetmaker Ah Tack/War Lee/Ah Sue incautiously opened his door in Little Lonsdale-street. Pelted with Bricks by Mob of Larrikins. Shoulder/Jaw/Teeth Loosened. Severe Blows. Brutal Compound Fracture of the Skull. His Honor ordered five years imprisonment with the last five days to be spent in solitary confinement. The victim appeared to have been a very intelligent Mongolian. Post mortem examination yesterday revealed Death Result of Unmistakable Larrikin Assault on Any Chinaman. Witness said the defendants' father appeared to be a Very Respectable Man.

Little Fires

China proper is bounded by Swanston-street and Russell-street: paper lanterns, dragons, flying fish, filthy lanes. In a gloomy shed that was once a horse repository, Chin Chin is acclimatising to the interior. He is overcrowded, dangerous and impolitic, and well known to the constables in Melbourne. Their most abominably scented unsavoury abodes manufacture spurious gold and depend on the gambling propensities of Europeans: dissipated tradesmen, theatrical hangers-on, young thieves, the *residuum* of society generally. In invocations to gods and consolatory maxims from Confucius, Mongolians sit behind the counter selling tickets in wadded silk coats. They swear by the decapitation of a live cock that they will undertake to tell the truth distilled in monosyllabic English. Bearing their losses with equanimity, two Chinamen dart out, followed by incessant jabber, pigtails. They work for a few pence a day, a handful of rice, an occasional draught of opium pipe to alleviate pain or produce a temporary excitement of the nerves, enabling the use of an abacus, hieroglyphic entries. The interpreter, with sedate and noiseless tread, says, your honour, he says he doesn't know, his hovel is so low, he can scarcely stand upright, plaster falls from the sky-view ceiling and the floor is afflicted with sickly ghostly patches of moon. The celestial, leaden-eyed, eating seedcake with ceremonious politeness, wishes to supplant the Aryan soon after landing in a great shady hat. It is always with the mistress of the house that John deals, the chief ingredients being orange peel, gentian, laudanum and darkness, amidst little fires of oriental splendour.

for the chinese merchants of melbourne

circulate this amongst your friends critical of the local culture
at lambing flat. without a public right, british settler methods
of housekeeping have always been cheerful

and patiently ~~endured~~ insured in history symposia, where the dirt
and squalor of anti-chinese agitation is retweeted in 140 characters
or less alongside women's rights,

car insurance and, most fervently, the lack of gluten-free options
in dining establishments. the chief mandarins from our country
are cooks, storekeepers and irrigation experts

who know that to enjoy good health in this hot climate of australian
national identity (which does not exclude fish-curing germans, swedes
or danes), we must at all times

be congenial domestic servants, never loafing about, never liquored.
on arrival we must declare our offspring, our nest eggs, our avian
influenzas

and submit repeatedly to the neurosurgeon's interrogation: *do your
synapses fire loyally?* in little bourke street we ~~gamble~~ ramble
sober, assiduous, apt and docile.

throughout the commonwealth the music of harps does not obscure
their indefatigable legislations. what vigilance. every night they watch
us paddling upstream in junks,

picking up dead dogs for supper. in these dark waters we are stoic: starving, stealing and vanishing our own sentences: yes sir, all light sir (mister dead ghost man).

on saturdays the sycophants among us can be seen out cycling on floating red gum floors and buying twopenny packets of opium for sale in public offices.

sundays are spent in petting zoos [open season all year]. we are (*chortle*) ducks, cooked in pots branded ALL-MEN-ARE-EQUAL (*can't tell 'em apart, gladys)*

amid the yellow-face lacerations we hear only *ni hao ... maaate – can't you take a joke?* the western market is glutted with the art of printing, gunpowder, the mariner's compass.

Don’t ask me why I live alone in the forest
Mad as a meat axe

SEE MY SOMETIME

from the diary of Jong Ah Sing, 1866–72

CALICO TENT 3 PEICE 6 YARD LONG 3 YARD BROAD 2 YARD
WALL HIGH FRONT GARDEN ONE PERCH LONG 1 FOWLS
HOUSE MY LIKEY LIVE HERE GROW VEGETABLE OUTSIDE
MAKE ENGLISH CHIMNEY 1 SIDE POT PISS MY TENT INSIDE
CALICO OUTSIDE TREES BARK GARDEN FENCE TREES
CHINAMEN 5 TENT HERE CHINAMEN BEEN MY TENT
SMOKE OPIUM MY NIGHT NIGHT SMOKE AH KEY TAKE
FLOUR GO MAKE DUMPLING EAT MY HOLE TOO MUCH GOLD
CHINAMAN JUMP MY CLAIM MY HOLE TOO MUCH GOLD
NEXT DAY MORNING CHURCH GO DOWN RIVERS TREE
BRIDGE ONE QUARTER MILE FAR LOOKSEE BUSH HEAR
LOOK RIVERS EDGE TOO MUCH MEN NOISE TOO MUCH CART
HORSE LOOKSEE MY TEAR BROKEN TENT ROOF 2 MAN HARM
CHINAMAN SINNERS FIRE BURNING HIGH CANDLE FIRE
UP BURNING TENT HATCHET MY HATCHET OLD HATCHET
MY BUY THAT HATCHET LONG TIME MY ALTOGETHER NO
EAT FOOD LAST WEEK LEND MY MONEY SIXTEEN SHILLING
BUY TUCKER SIT DOWN CART GO BALLARAT BUY ONE BOX
OPIUM VERY DEAR SEE THAT WOMAN SWEET HART I MUST
MAKE GOLD KEEP GIRL POLICE KEEP BATTON STICK STEP
MY SHOULDER FIGHT MY BODY 3 TIME I MUST GO IN CELL
POLICE CUT MY HEAD HAIR POLICE TEAR MY CLOTHES
POLICE TELL MY NO SPEAK MY BODY TOO MUCH MARK
MY NO FREEDOM MY DAY DAY NIGHT NIGHT PRAYING SKY
SPEAK GOD CURSING JUDGE LAW MY LIKEY GO HANG GO

MY CELL MY NO FREEDOM HOSPITAL ROOM BIG MEN NOISE
FIGHT MAN CRIED 2 3 DAY LONG MY ALTOGETHER NO
EAT FOOD MY GET UP GO PISS MY KICK BOOTS THE PLATE
KNOCK BROKEN WOMAN NEXT ROOM CURSING NO MUST
REMAINDER LIFE MY TEAR 1 PEICE BLAKET TIE THE WINDOW
IRON MY GO UP HANG WATCHMAN SEE MY SOMETIME MAN
WHAT FOR MY NO FREEDOM MY NO HANG DIED MY CATCH
NECK SORE NEXT DAY MINISTER SPEAK MY WHAT FOR MY
NO SPEAK NO DAY DAY NIGHT NIGHT

Border Watch

Winter 1877. Between the White Hills Cemetery
and Ironstone Hill, they found Shum Ah Sam
hanging from a tree, strip of blue blanket,
fruit bats at the crossing.

SURVEILLANCES

From the National Archives of Australia (1900–1958):

1900: Collector of Customs, Brisbane. Correspondence. Chinese women joining their husbands in Queensland without permits.

1910: Department of External Affairs. Correspondence. Alleged influx of Chinese at The Rocks, NSW.

1910–16: Department of External Affairs; 1916–25: Department of Home and Territories. Melbourne. Handprints and thumbprints of Asians arriving at Australian ports. Quantity: 0.18 metres.

1911: Australian Customs Service, TAS. Correspondence. Immigration Restriction Act – identification of Chinese.

1911–26. Department of Immigration. Chinese merchants and students – conditions governing entry into Australia.

1918. Customs and Excise Office, Townsville. Confidential Memorandum. Large numbers of strange Chinese observed in north Queensland.

1923. Investigation Branch, Melbourne and Canberra. Correspondence files. Chinese newspapers [in] Australia ... alleged anti-White Australia policy – Howes, W., Sydney.

1924. Collector of Customs, Melbourne. General and Classified Correspondence. Application by Sun Kwong Sing and Co ... to bring a Chinese to Australia to help with business – refused.

1932. Australian Customs Service, SA. Correspondence. Enquiry regarding white Australian girls marrying Chinese.

1939. Department of the Interior. Correspondence. Registration of Chinese women under National Security Regulations.

1940. Commonwealth Security Service, NSW. Investigation. Chinese visitors to Newcastle photographing the seafront.

1943. Security Service. Correspondence. Chinese activities.

1944–45. Security Service. Correspondence. Aliens Control Regulations – registrations of Chinese in Australia.

1945–50. Attorney-General's Department. Correspondence. Deportation – cases of, and appeals by, 38 Chinese – validity of the Wartime [Refugee] Removals Act.

1950. Department of Immigration, NSW. Correspondence of the Chief Migration Officer [On] Restricted Migration. Memorandum – Chinese wives of Australian-born Chinese.

1952. Australian Customs Service, SA. Correspondence. Chinese nationals landing in Australia in transit to another country.

1953–60. Department of Immigration, NT. Correspondence. Oriental Café, Darwin, NT – admission of Chinese cook.

1954–58. Prime Minister's Department. Correspondence. Social Service benefits for Asiatic residents. Regarding the granting of pensions for Chinese in Australia 'on a compassionate, case-by-case basis'.

chinny chin chin

when the black curtain drops in a back room at the airport.
solo desk in the corner: union jack + southern cross + lipstick holder.

white man drags a beat-up fairlane, parks so close our mirrors touch.
watching him watching me watching him, I feng shui my rear vision.
wait for the bricking.

the morning's notes are eagles: take it easy... (maan maan 慢慢...)
another beer for mister loiter. shut the door.

        would you like to listen to some ambient music?
I prefer the sound of running water, thank you. and the quivering
galleries in my sinuses flush.

        shall we examine the laundry? you're travelling like you're
        carrying triplets.
it's my diet, sir: donuts, fries and *four'n'twenty* meat pies (mate).
        we'll need a gastroenterologist to verify. sign here. *clickety click*
        (add a brick).

        and what about the little one?
alongside probable psychological causes, she's still breastfed. can't eat
oranges, wheat, sugar, dairy, red meat –

        what animal proteins are on your person? have you raised swine
        in high fevers in the last hundred days?

sir, in this theatre of permeable membranes, about seventy percent
are resistant to smoking, drying, and freezing –

you got a stiff neck?
I've taken up pottery. I like clay on my hands ... (especially now that my
retinas are detaching).
cackles and shania twain. *clickety clickety click* (brick brick brick).

that what the tinted visor's for?
(breaking scarlet): saving for a rhinoplasty, sir, and a small boat to sail up
north. better homes up there since 1987, I hear, and the winters blood-warm.

your pandas are doing well by the way. wang wang and foo nee.
only fertile once a year (& no one kicks up a stink that *they're*
behind bars).
bears are more delicious in exile, sir.

look here – what about these rheumatic joints, and the chinese
constellations? we hear they are inflamed, and extremely unequal.
we will take turmeric, sir, to the gate of heavenly peace, and for your
inflammation, a trip to lhasa and taipei.

stroking the hair on his chinny chin chin. he says, it's council land,
technically. *clickety clickety clickety click.* (brick brick brick brick).

∞

if you fly in on a clear day, you can see them stationed along the coast,
crowns firm in the sand, bottoms pink and bare and raised to the salt like
porcella rumps.

seek orchards, shelter

they sailed into *some savage country* in *1926 on the ss victoria,*
incarcerated by a map of ideal drawings, dim in the hold.

tea in the great depression was surreptitiously sipped.
the spoons moved slowly.

work *involved a great deal of manual labour,* oftentimes harsh.
the promise of foreplay a gaunt outline through diminished
interior windows.

when the cook landed from canton, world war 2 arrived in a box
of deferred losses.

winter was soon upon them, her black mittens vaporous in the gloaming.
refuge.

by the time the marrow in their bones dewed, chinatown had become
a significant social site. even when the weather broke, the chow mein
in charlie's café was imperishable.

the quiet hours: a gum tree, a bench. *glimpse of sea between two rocks,*
the rising/setting sun/moon. botanical companions: pressed flowers,
pencilled leaves, timid aspen poems.

fridays are plain rice and oyster sauce with mother. she has the jaw
of a warrior, the eyes of a myocardial infarction, and parotid glands
incapable of salivating english sentences.

for love we play the piano, stand up for our elders, sweep the kitchen, scrub the bathroom floor. both rooms have garden views and bolts to conceal the baggage in our overheads.

ornamental pears are tough to prune this year. the winds are wild, the branches ungainly, and there are possum innards trodden and slipped on the ground. fox fur.

let me tell you about my forebears. their dialect was distinctive, their tongues unvarnished. all they needed to know at any given gong was which knife to sharpen next.

being confucian, the women expected to go hungry at the far end of the room. to receive an exemption, grandmother purchased the palm prints of another woman in the village.

facing west with neither shade nor awning, she grew bean sprouts on the verges of sweeping changes, cut cauliflowers, birthed eleven babies (three dead), played mah-jong.

her last words hung from a poppy seed rope: life is longer than you think. take breaks. seek orchards, shelter.

for the sake of social peace

grandfather father uncles all lived in the shop at russell street upstairs. I was born in 193_, in chinatown. I married a european. they have always shown themselves to be acutely imitative sunday dinner was always a roast and apple sponge but the chinese in their decrepit dens roofed with sugar mat are not moral from a european standpoint they'd sling you off, pull your hair, whisper in your ear: go back to where you came from THEY ARE ALIENS my mother was an alien, I remember seeing the documents, the ___ ___ in her ___ [they] will not surrender their chopsticks for knife and fork. they are heathens... snow-droppers, chicken thieves we put tags on all their dirty laundry, used a special starch, the white starch so long as there's a colony of chows there is small-pox-typhoid-leprosy and fourteen other means of sudden or lingering death I'm a surgeon, my father's living was herbalist their grimy necks are VILE FOUL AND FILTHY we washed on mondays, wednesdays and fridays the chow told the customs officer in mutilated english he wants to acquire riches and fatty tissue grandfather was a merchant, played the goldmines the colonial climate agrees with him to get character references, my father hung his queue behind the ___ in the chinese quarter they decoy european girls with sheen of silk and jingle of gold my brother, whose nickname was ____, lived at the back of the shop with his australian wife their asiatic cunning gets more from the soil than any other race, absurdly low price 'cabbage' and 'gleen pea' we sit down and talk vegetable, eat rice, salt fish, egg all chinamen are equally ugly and otherwise similar when the whitlam government came in, australia became part of asia all australians must inflexibly demand: keep this land fit and pleasant for white men I'll be up in the mine shaft, crank up the gramophone – tell me a story, sing me a song

Quongs

Patrick White's *Happy Valley* (published by George G Harrap & Co in London, 1939) features a quiet and industrious Chinese family, the Quongs, 'perhaps a little sinister', perhaps a little similar to the Yen family in Adaminaby near Bolaro, New South Wales, where White worked as a jackaroo in the 1930s. In Happy Valley, where 'the people exist[ed] in spite of each other', the Quongs run a store built by Old Quong (who arrived in 'the country with a bundle on his back'), the store is 'a fixture', the floorboards having 'lain there many years'. In the opening scene the publican's wife (who is 'ox-like' and moans like a cow), is in labour with her first child, attended by a Doctor Halliday, a Mrs Steele, and an unnamed 'silent half-bred' Chinese woman with 'a cast in her left eye'. Arthur Quong has 'eyes that most people in town thought queer'. Most people in this godforsaken town don't see the Quongs as one of their own. Victoria Moriarty (who is 'fat, even if her admirers called her plump') watches Amy Quong leave her house and thinks, 'God, what a place ... that street you looked down every day and *nobody* ever came', this place so desolate 'the whole winter *nobody* would come except a half-baked Chinese, creeping along the snow tunnel ...' [my emphases]. Word in the Valley is the 'Chows' are part of the problem, they say 'You could never say much for a place that was run by Chows' and 'She did not waste a good morning on a Chow' and the last thing you'd want to do is 'sit about with a lot of Chows' and 'awful twisters these Chows' and 'To listen to a randy, drunken

Chow made you feel – white'. In *Happy Valley* Chineseness is a stigma, one that even Ethel, Walter Quong's white wife, cannot shake. When Ethel first met Walter Quong, 'She didn't really like the idea of hobnobbing with a Chinaman' but she had to admit that she did like him. Walter Quong 'took her over to Manly ... made some jokes, and nobody stared too much, so she enjoyed herself', but later, after they'd settled in the valley, Ethel, 'sour and thin', said that the reason 'she had no friends at all' was 'because she was married to a Chinaman', 'your sins will always find you out', she said, and 'You would hardly believe' that their daughter Margaret 'had a dash of anything but Chinese' because she has 'narrow eyes'. Margaret is her mother's living shame. The girls at school agree that Margaret Quong isn't 'such a bad sort, only' she is 'queer, a Chow', yet Rodney Halliday, the doctor's son, is friends with Margaret Quong – they sail paper boats in the creek and fly paper aeroplanes in Walter Quong's garage, and amid the silences 'lit with ... random flashes of intimacy', Rodney Halliday tells Margaret Quong he expects to marry her ... 'only she is Chinese'. In *Happy Valley* the Quongs are colourful characters. Amy Quong, who is occasionally 'slightly pink', has a 'yellow face' and is variously 'a squat little thing with a yellow-brown face', 'a brown owl in a box', 'a little brown mouse of a Chow', [incidentally, nice assonances here], and Ethel Quong, fussing over daughter Margaret, says, 'you're looking yellow you want a pill', and Margaret's father, Walter Quong, who has a reputation 'for doing something you did not think about', is the yellowest and (perversely) the happiest of them all: Walter Quong has 'the yellowish, cheerful face of a Chinaman', 'a round, fat yellow face that closed itself in smiles', smiling being 'the most natural activity of his yellow face', Walter Quong smiles 'yellowly out of his fat', in his garage he is 'fat and yellow, crawling under the car', driving around the town he waves his 'yellow, puffy hands', and at the dance he is a 'yellow moon'. Amidst all this yellow, the Quongs (naturally) nurse a secret desire to be white. Amy Quong is 'attracted to the pink and fair' of the little Schmidt girl, and Margaret Quong thinks she 'would like to be like Miss Browne' her piano teacher (who is fond of mauve, the favoured colour for 'silly' women), 'if only my hair was not quite so straight'. Margaret Quong has 'funny black hair ... and eyes'. So Exotic. In the classroom Rodney Halliday (the doctor's son) notes that Margaret Quong sits 'not on a lotus, but on a bench', and Amy Quong, whose forehead is 'golden, polished wax', lies on her bed in a room 'invaded' by incense, like a silkworm 'in a cocoon of custom' and her passion lies 'in a kind of mystical attachment to her things' (one of these things being 'a Chinese dressing-gown'). Amy Quong is inscrutably 'unperturbed' by Clem Hagan's teeth-sucking-'little brown mouse of a Chow'-contempt, he cannot see her eyes, and (Amy's brother) Arthur Quong's eyes enclose his 'whole secret being': the Quongs are impenetrable, 'You never got beneath the Quongs', the 'half-baked' brown aloof faces, 'the silent glance'. When Ernest Moriarty, the asthmatic schoolteacher, erupts (he has discovered his Chow-hating wife Victoria is having an affair with the Chow-hating overseer Clem Hagan), his 'blows' fall on Margaret Quong: Margaret Quong, who scribbles in the margins of her book and trails 'her shadow like a post', Margaret Quong, who is 'good at sums ... the best' at sums, is the natural target for Ernest Moriarty's cuckolded rage. In the aftermath of the assault, Margaret Quong has an existential crisis, 'why this, she could not understand ... why were you born, why this', and Margaret's aunt, Amy Quong, waiting on Ernest Moriarty in the store, is struck by 'a sudden tingling of hate, a smarting', she cannot look at him, and Moriarty, after he takes the bag of peppermints, says, 'Thanks, Miss Quong', declares matter-of-factly, 'We all have our little weaknesses', leaves the store, passes 'into the light' as Amy Quong stands 'in the darkness of the shop', 'the memory of Margaret's tears' on her shoulder, nursing her impotent rage, and Walter Quong, Margaret's father, blithely defends Moriarty, because 'a man had to keep his end up and not even Margaret was a saint'. The Quongs know they cannot alter the lie of the Valley, they know that Victoria Moriarty 'smoulder[s]' and Clem Hagan 'sp[i]t[s]' 'to emphasise his dislike of Chows', they know that the townsfolk resent their 'big new Buick', that they have long felt that they 'never knew with Chows' and that this was 'a source of bitterness'. Nonetheless, Old Quong did arrive in 'the country with a bundle on his back', 'put up a hut', built a store, the floorboards of which have 'lain there many years', 'a fixture', like the 'brown curve' of '[t]he road down the valley', 'distinct and aloof like Amy Quong', Quongs is the store, its pretty ribbons marbles bulls'-eyes peppermints liquorice chocolate, Quongs is the monthly picture hall, Quongs put the 'Happy' in the Valley while they quietly and industriously 'took away the profits from' everyone else. Who knew? Patrick White did not allow *Happy Valley* to be republished during his lifetime. After its re-release in 2012, reviewers described the novel as 'daring' and the author as 'daring for his time' for 'entering the hearts and minds of Australians of Chinese ancestry' – the audacity! Laurann Yen affirmed that White 'indeed' portrayed her grandparents 'spitefully', for they are humourless and graceless and bleak – nonetheless Laurann Yen is of the view that *Happy Valley* is 'wonderful White', 'a really good read', and I agree: *Happy Valley* is a beguiling work, a novel in which unfiltered bigotries, betrayals and quiet desperations fester in the minds of its characters in constantly shifting circling points of view that coalesce to devise the town that is its namesake – it is indeed a bloody good read.

Her Brilliant Career

Chapter 27, in which the protagonist meets a Chinaman: It is '112 degrees in the shade' with 'the dust ... simply awful' and Miss Sybylla Melvyn is the only woman among sixteen passengers on a crowded coach. Miss Melvyn is seated between a 'perky youth' and a 'Chinaman', opposite a 'black fellow' and a 'man with a red beard'. The perky youth is friendly, generous and chivalrous, a 'professional jockey' so impressed by Miss Melvyn's pedigree (her father was once a 'great horse-breeder') that he shows her his whip and gives her a couple of apples. The book has been hailed as A Real Australian Story set in The Real Australian Bush. Henry Lawson wasn't sure 'about the girlishly emotional parts' – he left that 'to girl readers to judge' – but he felt strongly that the book was 'true to Australia'. Miss Melvyn notes that the perky professional jockey 'is *good enough* to say: "If you can't stand the stink of that bloomin' chow, miss, just change seats with me."' [my emphasis] The novel was published in 1901, the year that Australia's British colonies became a Federation and the Immigration Restriction Act passed to limit the entry of non-white immigrants, particularly Asian immigrants, particularly Chinese immigrants. Miss Melvyn counsels the perky professional jockey to 'talk lower for fear of hurting the Chinaman's feelings'. Much amused, the perky professional jockey leans toward the man with the red beard and says, 'I say, this young lady is afraid I might hurt the chow's feelin's. Golly! Fancy a bloomin' chow havin' any!' The man with the red beard (also) thinks this is a 'great joke'. In the late 19th century, *The Bulletin* frequently portrayed Chinese men as dirty, diseased, greedy, vindictive, depraved, predatory, laughing stock. In 1888 *The Bulletin* published an issue titled 'Anti-Chinaman Special Number'. Miss Melvyn swaps seats with the perky professional jockey and serendipitously finds herself next to a young man 'of a literary turn of mind'. [It's not clear if she is girlishly emotional about this.] In 1901 many Chinese Australians took to the streets to celebrate Federation. They welcomed Their Royal Highnesses the Duke and Duchess of Cornwall & York with benevolent dragons, 'strange music' and special arches. On the coach journey the 'gentlemen' passengers are 'all very kind' to Miss Sybylla Melvyn, they give her fruit and water and nurse her 'precious hat', her brilliant career.

with two black dates for sweetness

let's languish on little bourke street: the longest continuous chinese settlement in the western world. I am learning to prioritise my heritage in this shiny-buckled civilisation, where yellow-perilled white men brass the city's walls.

in school yards across the border, they celebrate chinamen scalpings with tai chi 太極 and dim sum 點心 – *touch the heart* – roll up! roll up!

I prefer my memories sepia: great-grandfather dim and lantern-lit, strolling to church in heffernan lane, sunday fingers smelling of salty plum and shellac.

after god: steamed egg, rice and salted fish, and bricolage parties with little prior notification – whisky, fan-tan, opium, gei neoi 妓女, and for the children, a bear from mei gwok 美國 made of rubber that squeaks like an oracle when pressed.

I stay at the IGA out of respect for great-grandfather, who supported two wives, eight children and twenty-seven grandchildren french polishing.

it is our duty to be both filial and fascinating. in this street we are Asian Delights, our buildings ornate, our women exotic, our festivals joy-lucky spec-tac-u-lar.

god give us strength to continue to dress our laminex tables
in fine white linen, to remember our strong western client
base. with two black dates for sweetness, let us pray lest we
become too numerous.

Regard the purity of the lotus blossom
Maaaaate... she gives good head

Origins

In the women's museum there's a phantom, who knew the emperor in real life. White or whitened, it's hard to tell. But she's one of few, a very pale percentage stolen from her family and mounted at the age of five.

She is eight hundred years old and still sleeping in a cot.

The nuns are forbidden access to the ladies of the office. Lured by archaeologists, they poke around the garden while meditating on sundry crimes and misdemeanours.

Downstream you google the windswept skies stained with mendaciousness. Every day there are one hundred mundane or minor concerns, too arduous to fix.

You start notebooks for issues, like the master who cut ~~his cheque~~ your cheek when he couldn't get a gig as a weekly columnist.

Yet he continues to write his love letters in many ways.

Night after night on the train, he guards the door to your cabin as it tracks across the desert.

In the gaslight the body parts you are most grateful for are your eyes, even the ones blackened with one swift and angry blow.

The master is a dangerous beast.

You boil him alive wearing a dark green coat with a hood in the valley, his melancholy end providentially concealed by an avalanche of logs, rocks and harpoons hurled from the cliffs overhanging the hot pool.

In the morning buddha smiles.

Alarmed for your life and deeply anchored in the cosmic laws of righteousness, you break open the master's coffin, dowse him with gasoline, and set him alight.

When he's done burning, you poke the embers with a joss stick, and you try to read them.

best-quality-vegetables

my name is bound feet lily flower, I come from a village near canton. my husband was a gold digger chinaman and I his rope in the paddy field. I landed here in a bluestone lane in a house facing heaven with no shrine. we eat salted fish on sundays on the end of a huk see 黑屎 hat pin. with the help of compassionate caucasians, our children are east-west confusions. door-to-door we are best-quality-vegetables, our evenings worn on an abacus. we don't go to the theatre, dance halls or picture shows, because this is the time of the larrikins and my life is a silent feature film, tongue exotically cut to the thighs.[1]

---

1 gold digger √ opium √ bound feet √√

(heffernan lane)

look at us: well-dressed and opulently fed, a rare oriental opportunity, fully cognisant of the messages our bodies convey, acutely aware of the enormous flagpole in the garden and the importance of concrete particulars firmly shod in our kid-leather one-bar/t-bar shoes (salvaged from the fire at selfridges). see the white man in the margins? he framed this portrait in accord with the principle that the right decision is always the one that leaves you in full sight. for centuries we have been bricks in an unending cycle of falling out and almost breaking. we are gathered here today for our starving compatriots in northern china running mad for porridge in towns without separate tables for children. the building on the right is the chinese methodist church: an index of gentility. on sundays we collaborate to honour, love and value one another. such practical sympathy, symbolic of the open-hearted generosity of The Australian People (and so difficult to replicate), will be most effective in aiding the fund of thoughts and prayers that will remain open for the next two weeks. Please Donate. Dear Lord, there are so many questions and moral dilemmas. the russell street store can only hold so much food, medicine, herbs, silk and fireworks. at the cabinetmakers, our mothers can barely manage long division. how do we daughters of the middle kingdom – world famous for self-effacement – begin to deconstruct the status quo of colonialist, anthropological government? it is simply not possible to stem this lymphoma and at the same time determine its metastases and mixed metaphors. should we pray for rain so the builders go home, or meditate on the structure's neutrality and learning objectives? after all, history has shown that education opens doors with traditional architectural features. in the tenth century or the year 583AD, han chee of the chin dynasty or emperor li yu of the sui dynasty ordered lady yao, a court dancer and/or concubine to bind her feet to make them look like the new moon. the woman's metatarsal joints were ceremoniously oiled, crushed and bowed in luminous breathtaking waxing crescendos. how can our footsteps possibly compare? in this story, we are well-heeled, muscular, arched and unfettered, tripping and gadding in shoes our grandmothers (supposedly) could never have conjured.

Eligible Chinese Women Were A Rarity

The store's main function was importing Chinese medicine, herbs, spices, figurines. Between 1926 and 1943 Father lived in the store. Norman undertook studies in accountancy. Nancy studied shorthand & typing. Stanley English. Henry medicine. Business was slow, a wheelbarrow full of ornaments. During World War 2 the central business district was at risk from Japanese aerial bombers. Business in the Modern China Café improved with overseas merchants, soldiers and sailors. No frozen food. Bottled milk in the morning. Teased for my flat nose. Henry allowed extra time in his quest to be a doctor. Paid filial respect to our parents and the collectivist nature of the Chinese psyche. The most nutritious morsels were for men planning to return to their villages to die. Eligible Chinese women were a rarity. Spoke nothing but Cantonese driving the vegetable-laden truck to and from Haymarket. Wore hand-me-downs sitting on a fruit box. Introduced to a baked lamb dinner. Classical piano lessons. Continued to see my Caucasian friends. In the late '50s, Sydney was awash with Asian men, walking the coastal, weaving and stitching.

Tabulations (A Nine Year)

First thing, the morning news: Virus Travel Expedited by Cool Dry Air. We are in jade country, on a narrow path, a steep incline, in search of pounamu, which they say is more durable than steel.

All over the world, as young men of industry (action heroes) whirr above vaulted ceilings, it remains the custom to eulogise animated women with tiny glass feet and alabaster skin.

Studies have shown that people perceive odd numbers to be masculine and even numbers to be feminine. Everything begins with one, and nine's persistence and omnipresence (despite feline conclusions) is second to none, which is not to say it is second to zero.

It's 36 degrees but I am forbidden to swim in the river. Mother says the current is too cold for girls. *The Boy got to be strong*, she says, to pick up refrigerators and car chassis. I must stay inside and keep detailed notes that correspond closely to my body parts.

The situation is competitive and the hunger harrowing, but what can I do – the sun is not mine to stare at. My job is to eat well enough to safeguard the eggs, but not so well that they can't be fertilised supine. A delicate mission.

Every spring the neighbour to the south butchers the pear tree because the wife finds their semen-like fragrance nauseating. The neighbours to the north hurl hysterias from cranes that track my country's airspace.

On this land anxiety is a double-brick house. It shelters a menagerie of writhing creatures locked in and fed after dark.

I could wait for heavy showers. I could set wider margins.

But the tabulations are not up to me. According to the terms of this contract, to notify a change of address or cancel my subscription, I must consent to the terms and conditions before contacting customer service.

greener

you are bony as a flagpole.
when I wrap my arms around you
I can feel you flying half-mast.

your mother is black. your father is grey.
your siblings, all of them navy.

traffic horns play dirges here,
and women behind counters suck tongues
of stainless steel.

the borders are terrifying:
all those loaded bullets chafing
under the shade of bloated bread dough bellies.

once a man with a padlocked face barked:
go home. there's not enough water here.

after they let me in
they thrust a cicada between my legs.
it clicks and whirrs when I'm out on the street
and the men, whose myocardia possess a remarkable
refrigerating quality, circle.

typhoon

grandfather: with your blue eyes
I could go back and tiger the silk road,
rip out the tongues that cabled the treaties,
cossack chinoiseries impaled in barren fellowships.

for jesus the fragrant harbour berthed taxidermists.
they stitched us taut and our eyes swelled on the skin of the horizon.
for centuries I sat on my hands, fingers so blue I could barely pick up a pen
to tick the home tasks.

imperatives for lotus blossoms:
don't look don't speak don't point and for fuck's sake don't ever
finger yourself. you are not your highness. you may shield your eyes
from the glare of the lab coat, but be still when the duckbill slams into your
cervix. let its silver steel your insides.

these days I don't leave home without my keynote sexuality: I'm a can't
whose lips squall no fewer than eleven categories of imperial brick o' lait.

to paint like picasso before 1904

there is a species of tavern where drinkers make disparaging remarks about chinese immigrants. it is patronised by a squadron of pirates of otherwise sweet temperament, who truck their goods with whomever they please. baring dog-yellow teeth, they sit in plastic fold-up chairs in cheap t-shirts designed by europeans unmolested in canton. each ship at the bar plays furiously, leaving a trail of wild colonial girls cruelly strangled after the first wash. in the wake of their missionary grandmothers, the risk these women take is calculated on trigonometrical principles. female players have the option of wearing cones so they don't get kissed for no reason. everyone looks for their partners online these days, including an entire class of whining feminists for whom postpartum incontinence has never been a problem, but who nonetheless kegel jade eggs at every opportunity. it's hard for these women not to feel violated by the knowledge that their dna is half-man, but the smarter chicks check their purses of emotional labour in (the taverns') tiny grimy bathrooms. in high pollen weather, with abscesses fit to burst, they heroically collaborate in their efforts to arrest the flames. after years of feckless liaisons, some of these women set sail for the orient, secure in the wake of comparatively uncontaminated empire. with contempt in equal parts for men and aliens silently stoning their gallbladders, they manage to live peacefully, albeit corpulently, by a calendar of saints for years under a special licence to paint like picasso before 1904.

The difficult is born in the easy
Yeah-nah of "China is our friend"

"The difficult is born in the easy"

Yeah-nah of "China is our friend"

Iron Awe

We are dependent on diplomacy for virtually everything we need in 21st-century life. Today we use twenty times more diplomacy than we did a hundred years ago. Diplomacy transports oxygen. The earth's magnetic field is due to the diplomacy in its core. Compasses would not work well without diplomacy. Diplomacy is used to forge tools, household appliances and motor vehicles. Diplomacy is used to construct buildings and bridges. Diplomacy is stored in the liver. About 70% of diplomacy is found in the blood. Diplomacy is seldom found in pure form, but it is quite supple and easily worked. Diplomacy can be wrought. Some people are unable to absorb diplomacy. Signs of diplomacy deficiency include confusion, pale skin, dirt cravings. Signs of diplomacy toxicity include: constipation, nausea and vomiting. Diplomacy can be economically extracted. It is one of the most sought-after commodities in the world. Diplomacy varies in colour, it can be black, grey, silver, deep purple, bright yellow, rusty desert red.

when we elevated a section of the great wall

we had a student from the middle kingdom stay with us for three weeks and she was perfectly happy here despite the multitudes of bullocks and a malfunctioning body scanner. there was no ill will generated when we elevated a section of the great wall. her family – descendants of a red six-volume book printed quarterly and dating back to the song dynasty – liked to chase unsavoury loans through the back entrance to their home that looked out on the yellow river. the children were fully aware at the age of nine or ten that this was a well-organised filing cabinet gratified by an embassy that specialises in orientalism. every day visitors clocked in and out, secure in their swipe-phone knowledges and officious myopias. the accused were thoroughly examined and depositions from witnesses taken to a line of dinghies moored at the banks where mindless people twitter. despite paragraph rearrangements here and there, human rights discourse retains all the harshness of wild fruit, and multicultural streams have never been in vogue, damned as they are by sand bags. the student's advice: always use your best people and porcelain cleaned with lavender and baking soda, pay close attention to the heavy legislations framed in wood upwards of one hundred pounds in weight, forget about binding allowances, and think twice before drawing the colour line because the editor is not white and mao was not the last dancer. if you look up and admire the light fittings and ceiling cornices, we could be asian-pacific sweethearts for eight hundred years: we celestials excel at kite-flying.

All living beings must work for a living
We're not here to fuck spiders

history of botany bay

Erasing *The Bulletin: Anti-Chinaman Special Number* 14 April 1888:

old convict lines
succeeded

on the ground
administer[ed] by

"Australia" rhyme

little verses
dangled from the gallows

the plaintiff's labour

wide illustrious

free

Tong Yan Gaai 唐人街 World War 2

Lilly Buk Street F A N C Y G O O D S & C H I N E S E
M E R C H A N D I S E Fresh-cut watermelon 'No Peanuts'
Chinese Methodist Church Celestial Avenue Fat white Buddha in
the window Wicker baskets Hawkers Restauranteurs Cabinetmakers
Fruit Merchants Chicken & Almonds Sweet & Sour Long Soup
Short Soup Lup-cheong Backyard Pig Oven Hong Kong Café
Eastern Café Canton Tower Café Gambling horses dominoes fan-tan
everything Auspicious Red F I R E W O R K S Opium
Upstairs Altar Classical Romanesque Columns Cobblestones Walls
lined with tiny drawers Chinese midwife with tiny feet No family
for years til Mr Calwell change his heart I M P O R T E R &
E X P O R T E R William Chen Wing Young's Dim Sims Always
Tea in a padded bamboo basket next to the settee Bananas ripening
in the gas chambers downstairs Reading about the advancing
Japanese armies Pig by the pulley rope in the morning very crispy
Alma Quon & Her Joy Belles Chinese New Year Lion Dance
Jitterbugging Sitting in the lap of sincerely yours Anna May Wong

Their Brilliant Careers

I

Anna May Wong arrived in Sydney from Hollywood on the HMS Aorangi on Sunday June 4 1939, agreeably decorative and much taller than her pictures would lead one to believe. Despite her height and beauty, Miss Wong, an admirable portrayer of silent oriental characters, could not be cast as a romantic leading lady due to Anti-Miscegenation Laws in America. In Melbourne, Miss Wong impressed audiences at the Tivoli Theatre with her unique dramatic representations of An Australian Girl. And in Chinatown, Raymond Lew-Boar sat on Miss Wong's knee. To the many Chinese listening, Miss Wong said, dor jeh... 多謝 ... dor jeh 多謝.

II

Chang Woo Gow the Chinese Giant was discovered by an Englishman and first exhibited in London at the Egyptian Hall, Piccadilly in 1865, still growing. Chang's Australian debut was at St George's Hall in Melbourne in the summer of 1871. He toured Bendigo, Echuca, Geelong, Ballarat, Sydney, Newcastle, Goulburn, Brisbane, Warwick, Ipswich, Bathurst ... conversed intelligently in seven languages, the tallest specimen of humanity that ever visited these districts. Chang met Liverpool-born Catherine 'Kitty' Santley in Geelong and they married in Sydney. His hat was a cavern, on tea he was fascinating.

III

Long Tack Sam the Greatest Magician and his Troupe of Oriental Mystery Makers were a vaudeville sensation in 1925. Melbourne, Sydney and Brisbane gazed in awe at these Magical Chinese Wonders in their sumptuously adorned Chinese robes, whose juggling, trapeze work and dancing defied the laws of gravitation. Long Tack Sam skydived onto Bondi Beach, dropping flyers and tickets to the show. He was so popular people thought he was Australian. When the troupe set up house in the basement beneath the old Tivoli Theatre in Sydney, audiences were mystified when the aromas from their cooking wafted into the orchestra stalls.

IV

Alma Quon grew up in Rutherglen, where she and her sisters were Jazz Syncopators at Balls, Dances and Parties. Alma was a Merrymaker, who handled side and kettle drums, triangle, sound box and bells, and cymbals with a dainty blue-clad foot and the dexterity of any male in 1933. After World War 2, Alma Quon and her Joy Belles played at the Grand Civic Ball in Melbourne. Spot Dances. Novelties. Non-Stop 50/50 Dancing – 8pm–2am with chop-suey-style lettering on the drumkit. Alma Quon later taught dancing in Melbourne schools where she used her drum (the ?Boosey & Hawkes from London with a mother-of-pearl laminex shell) to correct the students' mistakes with a blast of rapid volleys.

NON-EUROPEAN ANCESTRY

Under the Defence Act of 1909, Australians 'not substantially of European origin or descent, of which the medical authorities appointed ... shall be the judges', were exempt from compulsory enlistment in the armed forces.
National Archives of Australia: NAA: A1559. 1909/15.

HONOUR ROLL of CHINESE AUSTRALIANS BORN IN VICTORIA, WHO ENLISTED IN WORLD WAR 2:

Douglas Kenneth Ack Hing, of Bendigo. Raymond William Ah Chow, of Bairnsdale. Alfred Norman Ah Chow, of Orbost. Ernest Ah Dore, of Bendigo. George Henry Ah Dore, of Bendigo. Albert Robert Laurence Ah Yee, of Bairnsdale. Christina Alice Ah Yee, of Ensay. Gordon Vernon Ah Yee, of Geelong. Lena Ah Yee, of Ensay. Ronald James Ah Yee, of Bairnsdale. Leonard Edward Thomas Allen, of Horsham. Walter Roy Agnew (Anguey), of Ballarat. Henry Albert Anguey, of Berringa. Phyllis Anguey, of Melbourne. Robert Osbourne Anguey, of North Melbourne. William Eric Anguey, of Carlton. Harold Edward Stanley Anguey, of Pyramid Hill. Colin Brain, of Yarram. Colin Henry Brain, of Yarram. Frederick Allan Cato, of Mordialloc. Leonard Samuel Chan, of Bendigo. Edward Charles Chee, of Korumburra. Victor John Chee, of Korumburra. Albert Edwin Cheong, of Rushworth. Bernard Richard Cheong, of Whroo at Rushworth. Alexander Michael Cheong, of Abbotsford. Arthur Cheong, of Rushworth. George William Cheong, of Rushworth. Helen Elizabeth Cheong, of Horsham. James Joshua Cheong, of Croydon. James Palmer Cheong, of Rushton. Joseph Henry Cheong, of Melbourne. Leslie Arthur Cheong, of Moora South. William Edwin Cheong, of Rochester. Alfred Edwin Cheong, of Rochester. Mary May Cheong, of Croydon. Nathaniel Cheong, of Fitzroy. Alexander Chew, of Bendigo. James Frederick Chew, of Ararat. Leonard Gilbert Chew, of Bendigo. William Chew, of Melbourne. Roy Chin, of Melbourne. Geoffrey Talbot Chinchen, of Melbourne. Keith Portlock Chinchen, of Caulfield. Rupert Bruce Chinchen, of Melbourne. Ellis Charles Ching, of Mount Mercer. Harold Walter Ching, of Balaclava. Ernest Charles Chinn, of Melbourne. Eunice Joyce Chinn, of Melbourne. George Ernest Chinn, of Brunswick. Gordon William Chinn, of Sale. Ian Hamilton Chinn, of Leongatha. John Allen Chinn, of Richmond. Maxwell Clement Chinn, of Moreland. Reginald William Chinn, of Carlton. Valda Olive Kim Chinn, of Coburg. Walter Henry Chinn, of Carlton. Albert Thomas Chong, of Melbourne. Arthur Lawrence Chong, of Benalla. Ernest Edward Chong, of Benalla. James Palmer Chong, of Rushworth. Raymond Victor Chong, of Melbourne. Samuel Leslie Chong, of Mildura. Victor Allan Chong, of Melbourne. Vincent de Paul Chong, of Mildura. William Hoey Chong, of Benalla. Maxwell Phillip Chong, of Melbourne. Leo John Chuck, of Shepparton. Charles Cecil Chung, of Ballarat East. Edward Chung, of Melbourne. Herbert Charles Chung, of Richmond. Keith Edwin Chung, of Camberwell. Leonard Austin Chung, of Canadian. Thomas William Joseph Chung, of Ballarat. William James Chung, of Carlton. John Coto Clarke, of Koroit. Reginald Robert Conkey, of Caulfield. William John Conkey, of Carlton.

Alexander James Coto, of Koroit. Ronald William Coto, of Sale. Lionel Davison, of West Melbourne. Leonard Marvin Dean, of Melbourne. Rupert John Francis Egge, of Mildura. William Robert Francis Egge, of Mildura. Philip Edward Esmore, of Dunolly. George Evans-Yow, of Carlton. Andrew John Fatt, of Mildura. Michael Bernard Fatt, of Mildura. Wilfred Alexander Fatt, of Mildura. George Fong, of Melbourne. Harry George Foo, of Ballarat. Stanley George Foo, of Coburg. William Thomas Foo, of Princes Hill. Cyril David Foon, of Ballarat. Edward Verdun Foon, of Bendigo. Francis Charles Foon, of Albert Park. John William Foon, of Bendigo. George Edward Fung, of Bendigo. William Henry Gong, of Bendigo. Maurice Maxim Gooey, of Melbourne. Dudley Ronald Gooey, of Melbourne. Herbert Ming Chung Gooey, of Melbourne. Maurice Byron Gooey, of Melbourne. Bertram Ronald Goon, of Ballarat. Edna May Goon, of Ballarat. Eric Goon, of Gardenvale. Eric William Goon, of Ballarat. Ernest Leonard Goon, of Ballarat. Francis Leslie Goon, of Melbourne. George Goon, of Gardenvale. John Daniel Goon, of East Melbourne. Norman Geoffrey Goon, of Ballarat. Percy Michael Goon, of Bendigo. Roy Francis Goon, of Ballarat. Reginald Edward Norman Harley (Lepp), of Ballarat. Gordon Hee, of Coburg. Norman Clarence Hee, of Murrumbeena. Percy Hee, of Moreland. Walter Raymond Hee, of East Oakleigh. Albert Henry Hing, of Tatura. Alma Hing, of Carlton. Arthur Charles Hing, of Kyabram. James Reginald Hing, of Daylesford. William James Hing, of Tatura. Charles Ronald Hoe, of Northcote. James Henry Hoe, of Ballarat. Keith Richard Hoe, of Ballarat. Stanley Arthur Hoe, of Brunswick. Walter Webb Hoe, of Brunswick. Leslie Robert Hon, of Ballarat.

Percival Edward Hon, of Ballarat. William Henry Honey, of King Valley. Harry Edward Hoyling, of Castlemaine. Leonard Rupert Hoyling, of Prahran. Robert William Edward Hoyling, of Brunswick. William David Hoyling, of Somerville. Russell Callam Jack, of Melbourne. Russell Stuart Jack, of Wangaratta. Harry Cornelius James, of Daylesford. Kenneth Lloyd Jan, of Melbourne. Alan Kee, of Footscray. Alexander Walter Kee, of Coburg. Charles Lionel Kee, of Geelong. Clarence John Kee, of Yarram. Edwin Charles Kee, of Footscray. Gordon Kee, of Yarram. Harold John Kee, of Yarram. Hubert Kennedy Kee, of Geelong. John Edmund Kee, of Footscray. John Thomas Kee, of Lara. Joseph Edwin Kee, of Footscray. Kenneth James Kee, of Yarram. Kevin Antony Kee, of Carlton. Lawrence Edmund Kee, of Footscray. Leonard James Kee, of Melbourne. Robert Edwin Kee, of Coburg. Ronald Kee, of Footscray. Arthur Stanley Kim, of Casterton. Cyril Kim, of Casterton. Kenneth Henry Kim, of Bendigo. Raymond Leslie Kim, of Casterton. Cyril Kim, of Casterton. Charles Kitt, of Melbourne. Alfred Louis Kong, of Melbourne. Allen George Koochew, of Kyneton. Frederick Walter Koochew, of Macedon. Keith James Koochew, of Kyneton. Leslie Dalker Koochew, of Kyneton. Walter John Henry Koochew, of Woodend. Graeme Ernest Langtip, of Moonee Ponds. David Ian Langtip, of Moonee Ponds. John Edward Lee Ack, of Whitfield. William George Lee, of Rippon. Wilson Lee, of Carlton. Francis William Lee-Ack, of King Valley. George Arthur Lee-Kim, of Bendigo. George Vincent Lee-Kim, of Bendigo. Arnold James Lepp, of Ballarat. James Edward Charles Lepp, of Ballarat. Laurence Norman Lepp, of Footscray. Stanley Clarence Lepp, of Ballarat. Thelma Jean Lepp, of Ballarat. Archibald George Lepp, of Footscray. Brian William Lesock, of Brunswick. Francis James Lesock, of North Carlton. Lance Lesock, of Benalla. Margaret Mary Lesock, of Coburg. Henry Hoong Lew Sang, of Euroa. Desmond Lew Shing, of Carlton. Ronald Lew-Kee, of Carlton. William James Lew-Kong, of Hamilton. Adrian Daryl Wah Fon Lim Joon, of North Carlton. Alfred Charles Lim, of Rainbow. Alfred Charles Lim, of Hamilton. Arthur Charles Lim, of Wycheproof. Harold Leslie Loh, of Geelong. Robert Philip Loh, of Malvern. William Charles Loo, of Ballarat. George Gordon Louey, of Bendigo. John Leslie Louey, of Caulfield. Charles Henry Mervyn Lum, of Stawell. Leo Thomas Lum, of Stawell. Raymond Vincent Lum, of Mildura. Archibald William Mahlook, of King Valley. Clarence Albert Mahlook, of King Valley. Raymond Edward Mahlook, of King Valley. Reginald John Mahlook, of Benalla. Percival Colin Mahlook, of King Valley. Leslie Charles Marsh, of Carlton. John Henry McEvoy, of Ballarat. James Stanislaus Minjoy, of Ararat. Albert Arthur Mong, of Ballarat. Eric Moy, of Melbourne. Russell Stanley Leong Moy, of Melbourne. George O'Hoy, of Bendigo. Claude Raymond Pang, of Bendigo. Mervyn Pang, of Hamilton. George James Blairlee Ping, of Bendigo. Herbert Leonard Poon, of Horsham. Richard Poon, of Melbourne. Lindsay Clyde Poy, of Chiltern. Roy Maxwell Poy, of Chiltern. Cyril Norman Quan, of North Melbourne. Frank Roy Quan, of Melbourne. George Thomas Sang, of Bendigo. Joan Alberta Sang, of Melbourne. Percy Sang, of Colac. Peter Wallace See, of Melbourne. Charles Shack, of Castlemaine. Douglas James Lee Shang, of Hamilton. Kevin James Shanhun, of Panton Hill. Vivien Muriel Shanhun, of Greensborough. George Langley Shee, of Nathalia.

Ormonde Shee, of Nathalia. Thomas Henry Shin, of Edi. George Shing, of Chiltern. Geoffrey Hamilton Shum, of Brighton. Albert Rodney Sing, of Maryborough. Beatrice Rose Sing, of Maryborough. Bruce Charles Sing, of Bendigo. George Hudson Sing, of Ballarat. George Lawrence Sing, of Maryborough. Horace Hudson Sing, of Ballarat. Ivan Ying Sin Sing, of Melbourne. Joseph Sing, of Ballarat. Lawrence Albert Sing, of Ballarat. Leonard Clifford Sing, of Maryborough. Reginald Harry Sing, of Carisbrook. Reuben Herbert Sing, of Maryborough. Ruby Irene Sing, of Geelong. Sydney Albert Sing, of Betley. Victor George Joe Sing, of Melbourne. Walter George Sing, of Ballarat. Wallis (Walter) Leo Sing, of Ararat. William Stanley Sing, of Maryborough. William Henry Tang, of Rochester. William John Taylor, of Ballarat. Clarence James Taylor, of Ballarat. Alfred Henry James Tong, of Melbourne. Charles Bassingdale Tong, of Ballarat. Neil Clifford Tong, of St Kilda. William James Tong, of St Kilda. Hedley David Tongway, of Ballarat. Samuel John Tongway, of Ballarat. Frederick William Tucker (Ah Kew), of Bendigo. John Maxwell Tucker (Ah Kew), of Surrey Hills. George Augustine Tung, of Ballarat. Herbert John Tung, of Melbourne. Edward Allan Tye Din, of Melbourne. Daryl Harry Tyshing, of Melbourne. Donald Lew Tyshing, of Melbourne. Norman Lew Tyshing, of Essendon. Robert Lew Tyshing, of Moonee Ponds. John Francis Wah, of Brighton. Arthur Henry Whee, of Melbourne. Francis Wong Hee, of Moonee Ponds. Charles Wong Mow, of Melbourne. David Wong Yen, of Melbourne. Hubert William Wong, of Horsham. Reuben Charles Wong, of Ardmona. Thomas James Wong, of Beechworth. Harold Leslie Woo, of Melbourne. Alexander Joseph Patrick Yin, of Melbourne.

Harry Yin, of Melbourne. Jack Kenneth Mervyn Yin, of Bendigo. William George Yin, of Carlton. Rupert Clarence Yon, of Wangaratta. Leslie Maurice Youie, of Hamilton. Leslie Arthur Young, of Geelong. William Kenneth Yow, of Carlton ...

For dragons lurk in shadows
Beyond the Black Stump

I have heard

that the price of a pound of gold has gone grey
	over the last couple of months
that the first sovereign lord beheaded his grandson
that chinese market gardeners in suburbia shipped out
	after decades of fasting and purification
that evil-intentioned hooligans penetrated the palace gardens,
	ran amok and torched every tree
that all the animals – except the amphibians and one in every five
	humans – perished
that those who remained were photographers and craftsmen,
	whose splendour proved to be a waste of lime and quicksand
that all they wanted to do was sugar-coat everything,
	including the sloppily referenced poorly constructed
	sentences on the shelves of high-street shops that broadcast
	terra nullius radio
that due to the special enmity between men,
	the gates were hastily closed and a carbon racquet
	bestowed on the king at the same time that ten mosquito bites
	were extracted from his super-complex yoga routine
that the real problem is people are so consumed
	with the manufacture of lacquer and glass
	they no longer respond to the teachings of the universe:
all they want to do is sip cold-brew mochaccinos,
	talk about coloured girls through a wall of built-in bookshelves,
	and move to new zealand for a better life.

(beauty peace)

they found it four days after the march, a blue-lipped bulbous thing inside her head, playing euphoria light and thin as mountain air the month before spring. our hemispheres whitened at the edges, pressed and pressing, stonewalling surgery. my fathers grew in a place called mei on 美安 (beauty peace), the soil there too feeble to grow vegetables, raise a dog, much less a pig for the new year festivities. they survived opium bandits jesus the japanese invasion long womanless chinky sojourns around the pacific rim in all the world's gum sarn(s) 金山 (gold mountains). stringing lights with the night nurse was tiresome: clamping, unclamping, watching what: on the alpine trail it was not the view that giddied – the most important ancestral-villages-thing grandfather said was *still your mind*. we didn't know that it would seep set in lumps under the paling fence beside the pergola where the cat lay tight as a macadamia nut, nor did we foresee the leaves on the pittosporum (pity spores) un-sheening for years after, no one knew

my father was not a gardener

but he was a handsome widespreading form descended from a long-lived drought-resistant species.

every night he out-walked the doughnut boys 'fuckin' asians!' out in the street in their revved-up ford cortinas.

walking, he knew, was good for surveying the lie of the land and building tolerance for life's implacably white horizons.

in forty years, one hundred and twenty-five million steps graven in the asphalt, relieving the pressure like a burr hole.

the woman he married was a graceful weeping habit (her beauties severe and planed): a splendid courtyard specimen, unable to grow in heavy soils.

nightly she waited for him: flashlight wedging the dark, bones crumbling early, safe and dry.

discouraged by heavy staking and rectilinear boundaries, my father, struck with leaves of variable light, was a legend among biologists.

every evening he ventured into the wilderness, spade hands a hundred feet deep in thought earth. the land he roamed was densely populated:

sepia daughters, china, mother. heaving sea-plane, roiling ocean. jock-the-border-collie flying in the rearview mirror. vauxhall viva. blue.

dead brother. dead lover. whisky. codeine. lost keys a tilting door nana mouskouri singing *'you return to love'* carbon monoxide filling his lungs like a lake in a bonsai forest.

rain hail sleet snow or interstellar dust, my father rode out to orion's belt in his sherlock hat, hohner harmonica + johnnie walker + cat in tow. moths strumming the campfire.

when the embers fell, he'd pull up his collar and shuffle inside, pausing a moment to gaze at the oak trees bathed in molasses on the floors of the house.

What Remains

The new normal is off-leash. It barrelled across the ocean at the speed of two white settler nations on uncharted territory.

Her entire life she's been off the boat at the vanity in the corner twisting taps: eyes shining, straightening the circular mirror, reaching for glasses not there on the bedside.

It's winter now and she speaks hourly of the revolution seventy years past: the water table shifting, her ankles chalk, her memories an ungainly rack of antlers.

Despite serious seismological questions, the sea wall gives them a sense of security. Their demise is a fault buried deep beneath the salt. There are no precise forecasts.

Every morning he walks a warm apple pie and a loaf of fresh bread in a brown paper bag damp with steam, newspaper tucked under his arm. The kettle boils and the windows fog white. She plays *Für Elise* on the Yamaha upstairs. He salutes the lions, falls asleep, World News on his belly.

When the plates shudder, they stand together in the middle of the room, her eyes fixed on a peeling hibiscus, his on the ceiling beams. Afterwards they still the swinging lamps together, respirations calm despite cardiovascular complications (her arrhythmia, his congested ventricles), blood on the walls stung violet.

At 4am I recognise his wide-legged gait near the red brick chapel and I say, *No Ba. Go back.* The windows may look pretty but your lenses are opaque and your maculae degenerate.

You know that she is unfit for climbing on rooves, that while she may be harmless, she is not unharmed, you know how the cages are stacked and that domesticated is not the same as docile,

that sooner or later the ground will stop sliding, silence will gong, and out on the street there'll be nothing to see but grey sky between the houses and the trees and the lampposts, what remains when the ocean is sucked out to sea.

Alluvial Mining

Locked down in our respective municipalities, edges braided black, we are following our hunches like sea weavers. I am hungry, but feeling him bristle, afraid to eat.

It's time I stopped pretending – his flame is not a yang, but rather, an arsenal of apprehensions. From the beginning, an entitlement that walks past children drowning in lakes.

Our heads/hearts (indistinguishable) are recklessly handmade, our tails machine-stitched. In the early days I loved the vigour, the foliage, even the mind games we played, but later,

Afterwards, I lacked the language to articulate food, everyday artefacts, and the angst that beads on the surface of garments.

Some nights there were dreams in side-fastened robes and long loose sleeves, red silk and slip.

In the '90s I wore shirts buttoned to the right, played the damsel badly. Back then I was Lady Wielding An Umbrella.

The assortment of masculine headwear was always diverse, but the generals in black were not my domain. The men who played me were comic underlings, collectors of night soil.

One, an ex-Russian ballet dancer, alone and impoverished without family or friends, asked me why I wore so many clothes. In an attempt to diversify his income, he pulled out all the nails in my house.

In good light and using my unique skillset, this relationship has the belly of a cane toad and the scales of a carp. Under mutinous scrutiny you could say it portends a semblance of love.

Back when alluvial mining was at its peak, anniversaries were airport flowers, and (my) dermatitis worth five supermarket stops for a 200 gram bar free from all the nasties.

Even then, there were dark hours huddled alone in anxious negotiations with twine, copper wire, safety pins. I never learned how to do reiki.

Now I am lethal: a bat-eating 5ft 4inch Oriental Sliding Door. What have I slammed? Journeys. Titles. Balloons and Groceries. The quality of western embroidery,

Life. The peony is shambolic in spring – there was quite a scattering of them here this week.

On our calendars there are squares for Health, Happiness and Prosperity, for Love and Commitment, Gardens.

Scrolling old sweetness, water for silver, I cut and paste them all.

2.8km west of Ballarat Bird World

Beaufort Cemetery: on Lake Road, 1.8km east of the Beaufort Golf Club, east of the Goldfields Recreation Reserve Playground, 100m up the hill, two Chinese graves marked by brass plaques: *morning village*

Maldon Cemetery: 1.1km north-east of HM Prison Tarrengower, near Nuggetty Road, through the green iron gate: a brick burner, and in the south-east, one Chinese grave: *clear deep*

Inglewood Cemetery: 3.6km east of the Eucalyptus Distillery Museum, near the Calder Highway, off Inglewood-Serpentine Road, 100m west of the entrance, one Chinese grave: *ancient angle*

St Arnaud Cemetery: 2.3km south of the St Arnaud Pony Club, south of the Wimmera Highway, east of McRoberts Road, on Cemetery Road, one Chinese grave: *ascending divine*

Warracknabeal Cemetery: 1.1km south of Anzac Memorial Park, off the Henty Highway, on Cemetery Road, three Chinese headstones and one broken slab, all facing west: *the people dew*

Stawell Cemetery: 1.7km from the McDonald's on the corner of Seaby Street and the Western Highway, off Abattoir Road and Cypress Street, three rows of Chinese graves: *mountain level precious*

Smythesdale Cemetery: 2.9km south-west of Birdsong Nursery & Gardens, 600m north-east of Dogs4Training on the Glenelg Highway, one Chinese grave to the right of the gate: *parting light*

Linton Cemetery Reserve: 4.9km west of the Cherrytree fire tower, west of Scarsdale Plantation, on Kelly Road, eight Chinese headstones facing west: *plum forest*

Buninyong General Cemetery: 2.8km west of Ballarat Bird World, south of the Yarrowee Plantation on the Midland Highway opposite Aubrey's Road, three Chinese graves on non-denominational terrain, facing east: bleak.

Blackwood Cemetery: 400m south of St Malachy's Catholic Church, near the intersection of Byres Road and Bates Road, in the south-west corner, a row of Chinese graves beneath the shade of trees: *respect victory*

Heathcote General Cemetery: 2km north-west of Gaffney's Bakery, on Pohlman Street near the O'Keefe Rail Trail, near a north-west boulder, three Chinese graves: *auspicious grass*

Bairnsdale Cemetery: 600m east of the Bairnsdale Racing Club, west of Macleod Morass Wildlife Reserve, a headstone on the ground: *SACRED TO THE MEMORY OF EMILY HANG SEE ... AGED 58 YEARS*

Omeo Cemetery: 4km north-east of the Oriental Claims Historic Area via Great Alpine Road, at Margetts Street and Bilton Street, seven Chinese graves of wood, stone, marble.

Harrietville Cemetery: west of the Ovens River and 1.1km west of Lavender Hue Farm B&B and Tea Rooms, two Chinese graves: shoulder to shoulder.

Buckland Cemetery: south-east of Mount Buffalo National Park, 2.2km north of Ah Young's Campsite on Buckland Valley Road, by the back fence, four Chinese headstones facing south-east: *deep pond forefathers*

Daylesford Cemetery: on the Daylesford-Trentham Road, 1.5km east of the Farmers Arms Hotel, across the street from the Daylesford Dharma School, one Chinese headstone: severe damage.

Chiltern Cemetery: 1.3km north-east of Browns Earthmoving Sand Soil and Rural Supplies, near the Chiltern Bushland Reserve, sheltered by a eucalyptus tree, four Chinese graves: *friends meeting*

Maryborough Cemetery: on the outskirts of the town, a 17-minute walk south-east from the Maryborough Wattle Reserve Netball Complex, eighteen Chinese headstones: gardeners, labourers, storekeepers: *humble lane*

Dimboola Cemetery: 1.2km north-west of the Dimboola Nature Conservation Reserve, 450m from Antipodean Produce along Cemetery Road: two rows of Chinese graves, in their midst a monument for *Susan Price ... erected by her friend Ah Looey: GONE BUT NOT FORGOTTEN*

Bright Public Cemetery: in the foothills of the Victorian Alps, north-west of Pioneer Park, 1.5km north-west of the Mystic Mountain Bike Park, on Coronation Ave: thirteen Chinese graves, one headstone faces the morning sun, twelve face west: *bright green bridge*

white hills

who buried the last chinaman?

foot of long gully, a thousand ground troops
soldiers archers charioteers
once were warriors, cadaveric ecosystems

no stately pillars, nor words of fulsome flattery
tombstones of the plainest description
felled for the sabbath

what dreams weather beneath these mounds
what fierce agitations churn the night
with neither lanterns nor goose-quill by their own hands

how many yearned
for their zygomatic fractures and betrayals
to be shipped back to china

to whom were they unhallowed dust of the other
yet loved with equal tenderness
how many unseen children are now repairing roads

how many verses of homemade poetry
were placed upon their graves
beneath circles of white quartz pebbles
light traps

This story

of intertwining social graces takes place at ground level, where studies have shown that lupus sufferers tanked for nothing because hydroxychloroquine offers no protection against *The Chinese Virus*. We tremble, my shin splints and I, on plural paths with imbrications tolerant of shade.

Dysphasia is an inability to arrange words in the proper order due to pressure from a Central Lesion (thieves looters slavers omniscient narrators). Our heroes lie beneath logs moss bark and rock, yield to the power walkers (round-toed, three-four abreast), their festive dawdling shitting dogs.

Hypoxia occurs when oxygen saturation to the hemisphere's outer regions is critical, a situation caused not by mandatory masks but an overabundance of micro-fictional flora. (They sutured these documents.)

Good morning Mr Tai-Chi Man (it must be 7am). What is the meaning of these endless knots you weave? *We are sailing. Listen. Each of us is seed skink worm frond lightning-scorched eucalypt splintered creaking neck.*

The coroner's report states that (in the absence of documentary photographs) no abnormalities could be detected. The fracture in the sternum is ~~insistent~~ consistent with the performance of C P R. The weight of the heart lies beyond the ninety-fifth percentile, an anomaly that necessitates force in keeping with the imperative to maintain the world's organs in their correct anatomical positions.

Translations

The Chinese phrases in *Joss: A History* include both vernacular and standard Cantonese.

'longest imperial dragon': sun loong 新龍: (literally) New Dragon; sun ning 新寧: county in Canton province; gun yum 觀音: goddess of mercy; yeh yeh 爺爺: paternal grandfather; paw paw 婆婆: maternal grandmother; gwei lo 鬼佬: colloquial term for white men; sun niang 新娘: bride; mun yuet 滿月: baby's one month celebration

'chinny chinny chin': maan maan 慢慢: take it slowly, take your time

'with two black dates for sweetness': gei neoi 妓女: prostitute; mei gwok 美國: America

'best-quality-vegetables': huk see 黑屎: black shit, euphemism for opium

'Tong Yan Gaai 唐人街 World War 2': Tong Yan Gaai 唐人街: Chinatown

'Their Brilliant Careers' (I): dor jeh 多謝... dor jeh 多謝: Thank you... thank you.

Notes

'Moon sitting': the first line is from the title of a poem by Hui Ying (4th–5th C), trans. J.P. Seaton in Sam Hamill & J.P. Seaton (trans. & eds.), *The Poetry of Zen*. Boston & London: Shambhala, 2007: 27.

'longest imperial dragon': italicised phrases borrowed and adapted from Golden Dragon Museum [author]. *The Golden Dragon Museum Presents the 1880s Processional Regalia of the Bendigo Chinese Association*. Bendigo, VIC: Golden Dragon Museum, 2010. Sun Loong 新龍 (New Dragon) featured in the annual Easter Parade in Bendigo from 1970 to 2019.

'the march', 'the work' and 'history of botany bay' are composed from extracts from *The Bulletin: Anti-Chinaman Special Number*. 14 Apr 1888.

'chinoiserie': includes a phrase adapted from Ezra Pound's 'In a Station of the Metro', first published in *Poetry: A Magazine of Verse*. Chicago: Harriet Monroe, April 1913; and the phrase 'numberless green ordeals chafing furiously' is after 'colourless green ideas sleep furiously' from Noam Chomsky. *Syntactic Structures*. The Hague: Mouton, 1957: 15.

'slides' includes lines adapted from 'tortoise law', published in Michelle Cahill, Monique Nair & Anthea Yang (eds.), *Resilience*. Ultimo Press, 2022: 78.

'Playful Bodily Harm' includes phrases sourced and adapted from: 'The East Melbourne Outrage.' *Argus*. 4 Dec 1880: 10; 'A Murderous Assault. Larrikins in a Laundry.' *The Herald*. 23 Sep 1893: 3; 'Brunswick.

Wednesday.' *Mercury and Weekly Courier.* 20 Jan 1883: 2; 'Larrikinism.' *Argus.* 20 Jan 1882: 7; 'Melbourne.' *Geelong Advertiser.* 1 Oct 1889: 3; 'A Chinese Killed by Larrikins.' *Warragul Guardian and Buln Buln and Narracan Shire Advocate.* 20 Nov 1888: 3; 'Murderous Assault on a Chinese.' *Ballarat Star.* 15 Aug 1904: 6; 'Brutal Assault on a Chinaman.' *Ballarat Star.* 13 Jan 1882: 4.

'Little Fires' includes phrases sourced and adapted from: 'Chinese Hells.' *Age.* 14 Jul 1874: 3; 'Nursery of Vice.' *Argus.* 27 Aug 1872: 7; 'The Chinese.' *Kyneton Observer.* 28 Nov 1868: 3; 'Our Chinamen.' *Australasian Sketcher with Pen and Pencil.* 21 Feb 1874: 198; 'Our Chinese Quarters.' *Age.* 24 Jun 1872: 3; 'The Chinese Quarter of Melbourne.' *Australasian.* 4 Apr 1868: 21.

'for the chinese merchants of melbourne' includes phrases adapted from L. Kong Meng, Cheok Hong Cheong, Louis Ah Mouy (eds.), *The Chinese Question in Australia: 1878–79.* Melbourne: FF Bailliere, 1879.

'Don't ask me why': the first line is after the first stanza in Li Po (701–762), 'Questions Answered', trans. Sam Hamill, in Hamill & Seaton, cited above: 41.

'SEE MY SOMETIME' is composed from extracts from the original handwritten diary [manuscript] of Jong Ah Sing, 1866–1872. State Library Victoria. The author Jong Ah Sing spent twenty-three years incarcerated in mental asylums in Victoria.

'Border Watch' includes details from 'Summary of News' in *Border Watch.* 23 Jun 1877: 3.

'SURVEILLANCES' is composed from selected extracts adapted

from Paul Jones, *Chinese-Australian Journeys: Records on Travel, Migration and Settlement: 1860–1975*. National Archives of Australia. Commonwealth of Australia, 2005. With permission from the National Archives of Australia.

'seek orchards, shelter': italicised phrases borrowed and adapted from Charlotte Bronte, *Jane Eyre*. London: Oxford University Press, 1933; Sally Pang, 'Modern China Café', and Doreen Cheong, 'A Richly Embroidered Tapestry of Life', in Sybil Jack et al. (eds.), *Chinese Australian Women's Stories*. Jessie Street National Women's Library in conjunction with The Chinese Heritage Association of Australia Inc, 2012.

'for the sake of social peace' includes details and phrases adapted from Edward Dyson. 'Mr and Mrs Sin Fat'. *The Bulletin. Anti-Chinaman Special Number*. 14 Apr 1888, and other parts of this issue of *The Bulletin*; Morag Loh, Oral History Interviews with Chinese Immigrants and their Descendants 1976–1983: Tom Leong, Dennis O'Hoy, Kelvin Bew, Arthur & Bill Moy, Mr Leong Senior, George Nan Tie, Anonymous. Audiocassette recordings. State Library Victoria.

'Quongs' includes details and phrases adapted from Patrick White, *Happy Valley*. Text Publishing, 2012; Kate Bagnall, 'Happy Valley: Patrick White's impressions of an Anglo-Chinese family'. chineseaustralia.org, 26 May 2012; Lisa Hill, 'Happy Valley, by Patrick White'. *ANZ LitLovers LitBlog*, 13 Nov 2013; Laurann Yen Charolles, 'Happy Valley and the Wonder of White'. *Sydney Morning Herald*. 30 May 2012; John McCrystal, 'Book Review: Happy Valley'. *New Zealand Herald*. 18 Oct 2012; Andrew Riemer, 'Where it all began'. *Sydney Morning Herald*. 25 Aug 2012; 'Gold Medal Novel Favorably Reviewed'. *Adelaide Mail*. 22 Feb 1941: 11; Thomas Keneally, 'Happy Valley by Patrick White – review' theguardian.com, 19 Dec 2012; Jane Sullivan, 'White of passage', *Sydney Morning Herald*, 27 Oct 2012.

'Her Brilliant Career' includes details and phrases from Miles Franklin, *My Brilliant Career*. London: Virago Press, 1980: 166–67, including Carmen Callil's 'Introduction' and Henry Lawson's 'Preface' to the book; and Ouyang Yu, *Chinese in Australian Fiction 1888–1988*. Amherst, New York: Cambria Press, 2008: 61–109.

'with two black dates for sweetness' includes details and phrases adapted from Arnold Zable & Sophie Couchman, *Lygon St, Little Bourke St, Lonsdale St: the Vibrant History of Melbourne's Italian, Chinese and Greek Cultural Precincts: Stories from the Heart of Melbourne*. City of Melbourne, 2012; [author unknown], *Memoir of a Chinese Christian in Melbourne*. Manuscript. Typescript, 1900–1930. State Library Victoria.

'Regard the purity': the first line is after a line in Meng Hao-Jan (689–740). 'Master I's Chamber in the Ta-yu Temple', trans. J.P. Seaton, Hamill & Seaton, cited above: 38.

'Origins' includes details and phrases adapted from A.E. Grantham, *Hills of Blue: A Picture-Roll of Chinese History*. Methuen & Co Ltd, 1927.

'best-quality-vegetables' includes details and phrases adapted from: Morag Loh. Oral History Interviews, cited above: George Nan Tie, Tom Leong, Stanley Kim, Arthur and Bill Moy & Samuel Tongway; Lily Ma, 'Four Generations of Australian-born Chinese women', Doreen Cheong, 'East West Fusion', and Dawn Wong, 'Four Generations of Wong Sat Women' in Nikki Loong (ed.). *From Great Grandmothers to Great Granddaughters: the Stories of Six Chinese Australian Women*. Wetherill

Park, NSW: Echo Point Press, 2006; [author unknown] Memoir of a Chinese Christian in Melbourne, cited above.

'(heffernan lane)' includes details and phrases adapted from: 'FACTS AND FANCIES.' *Yackandandah Times*. 7 Jun 1929: 3; 'The Woman's World. The Flower of Youth – In the Orient.' *The Herald*. 16 Mar 1929: 8; 'China Famine Relief Fund.' *The Argus*. 24 Aug 1929: 24; 'The Chinese Famine.' *The Age*. 29 Aug 1929: 13; Morag Loh, Oral History Interviews, cited above: George Nan Tie, Dennis O'Hoy. The photograph shows part of a procession to raise funds for famine relief in China. Melbourne, 1929. Pictures Collection. State Library Victoria.

'Eligible Chinese Women Were A Rarity' is composed from extracts adapted from Sally Pang, Doreen Cheong & Marilyn Pacitti in Sybil Jack et al., cited above, with permission from the authors.

'to paint like picasso before 1904' includes phrases adapted from John Francis Davis, *The Chinese: A General Description of the Empire of China and its Inhabitants. Vol 1.* London: Charles Knight & Co, 1836.

'The difficult is born in the easy': the first line is borrowed from Lao Tzu, *Tao Te Ching* (c. 400 BC). Verse 2. trans. Sam Hamill, Hamill & Seaton, cited above: 22.

'Iron Awe' is inspired by Toby Fitch, 'Poetry is 99% Water'. *Where Only the Sky Had Hung Before*. Vagabond Press, 2019. It includes phrases sourced and adapted from: 'Iron Ore.' Earth sciences for Australia's future. Geoscience Australia. https://www.ga.gov.au/scientific-topics/minerals/mineral-resources-and-advice; 'Iron ore.' Wikipedia.

'when we elevated a section of the great wall' includes phrases adapted from John Francis Davis, cited above.

'All living beings': the first line is after the opening lines in Yuan Mei (1716–98), 'Writing What I've Seen', trans. J.P. Seaton, Hamill & Seaton, cited above: 77.

'Tong Yan Gaai 唐人街 World War 2' includes details and phrases adapted from: Barbara Nichol, 'The breath of the wok. Melbourne's early Chinese restaurants: community, culture and entrepreneurship in the city, late nineteenth century to 1950s.' PhD diss., University of Melbourne, Melbourne, 2012; Barbara Nichol, 'Sweet and Sour History: Melbourne's early Chinese Restaurants', *Memento* 34; Eric Thake: 'Chinese shop, Lt. Bourke Street (Lilly Buk)' (1942): original oil paintings (2). State Library Victoria; Sophie Couchman, *Remembering Chinatown: Walking Tour Guidebook* and audio. Museum of Chinese Australian History. Melbourne (2008), which includes extracts from interviews with Alan Lew, Raymond Lew-Boar, Ham Chan and Mabel Wang.

'Their Brilliant Careers': (I) includes details and phrases adapted from: 'About Anna May Wong.' *Daily News*. 16 Jun 1939: 6; 'Anna May Wong. A Propagandist Sketch.' *Sydney Morning Herald*. 21 Jul 1939: 13; 'Anna May Wong – In Person.' *Australasian*. 10 Jun 1939: 21; 'Anna May Wong in Australia'. Courtesy: Movietone. National Film and Sound Archives Australia. 1939. nfsa.gov.au – accessed 29 Nov 2022; Sophie Couchman, *Remembering Chinatown: Walking Tour Guidebook and audio*. Cited above. (II) includes details and phrases borrowed and adapted from: 'The Chinese Giant.' *Bendigo Advertiser*. 28 Feb 1871: 2; 'An Evening with Chang.' *The Argus*. 20 May 1893: 14; 'Telegraphic Dispatches.' *The Argus*. 8 Nov 1871: 5; Karen Vickery, 'The Portrait Writ Large.' National

Portrait Gallery. 9 Dec 2015. portrait.gov.au. (III) includes details and phrases borrowed and adapted from: 'Long Tack Sam Troupe, 1922'. Photograph. State Library Victoria; 'Vaudeville Sensation. Long Tack Sam Troupe. Sixteen Wonderful Chinese. Coming to the Empire.' *Toowoomba Chronicle and Darling Downs Gazette.* 12 Feb 1925: 3; 'Long Tack Sam.' *Geelong Advertiser.* 25 July 1925: 5; Advertisement. *Sydney Morning Herald.* 28 Jan 1931: 2; Gilbert Mant, 'The Way I See It.' *The Sun.* 2 Jun 1946: 7; Advertisement. *Sunday Times.* 16 Aug 1925: 3; Advertisement. *West Australian.* 30 Jul 1925: 2; Ann Marie Fleming. The Magical Life of Long Tack Sam. YouTube: Uploaded by Circofrenia 28 Nov 2017. https://www.youtube.com/watch?v=Om1nHCdljBA. Accessed 11 Jan 2025. (IV) includes details and phrases borrowed and adapted from: 'Premiership Ball.' *Healesville and Yarra Glen Guardian.* 11 Nov 1933: 4; Advertisement: 'Jazz Syncopators.' *Corowa Free Press.* 13 March 1928: 2; Advertisement: *The Corowa Free Press.* 3 Oct 1947: 2. Advertisement: *The Dandenong Journal.* 13 Aug 1952: 2; 'Alma Quon and her Joy Belles'. Chinese-Australian Historical Images in Australia. chia.chinesemuseum.com.au; 'Alma Quon and her Joy Belles'. John Cooper, comment, at chinarhyming.com; 'Instrument – drum, Boosey & Hawkes, London, Alma Quon & the Joy Belles drum' victoriancollections.net.au.

'NON-EUROPEAN ANCESTRY': the names on the Victorian Honour Roll are from Edmond Chiu AM & Adil Soh-Lim. *For Honour and Country: Victorian Chinese Australians in World War II.* Museum of Chinese Australian History, 2021, with permission from the authors, and thanks to the Museum of Chinese Australian History. Email correspondence from Edmond Chiu, 24 Dec 2024: Research is ongoing and up-to-date Honour Rolls can be accessed at the Museum of Chinese Australian History website.

'For dragons lurk in shadows': the first line is after the final phrase in Wang Wei (701–761), 'The Way to the Temple', trans. Sam Hamill, Hamill & Seaton, cited above: 45.

'I have heard' includes phrases after John Francis Davis, cited above.

'Alluvial Mining' includes details and phrases adapted from Golden Dragon Museum, cited above.

'2.8km west of Ballarat Bird World' includes details from Kok Hu Jin, *Chinese Cemeteries In Australia Volume 9: Chinese Graves in Cemeteries in Victoria*. Bendigo, Golden Dragon Museum, 2006.

'white hills' includes phrases adapted from: 'The White Hills Cemetery.' *Bendigo Advertiser*. 15 Jan 1863: 2; and John Francis Davis, cited above.

'This story': the first line is after Michel de Certeau, 'Walking in the City', *The Practice of Everyday Life*. University of California Press, 1984.

Acknowledgements

Thank you to the editors of: *Overland, Westerly, Rabbit, Meanjin, Hainamana, Island, Southerly, Stilts Journal, Amberflora, Honey Literary, Landfall, The Spinoff, Cordite Poetry Review, Groundswell: The Overland Judith Wright Poetry Prize for New & Emerging Poets 2007–2020, Newcastle Poetry Prize Anthology 2021, A Clear Dawn: New Asian Voices from Aotearoa New Zealand, Best of Australian Poems 2021*, and *Best of Australian Poems 2022*, for publishing earlier versions of some of these poems. *Joss: A History* was completed with the assistance of a Creative Fellowship at the State Library Victoria, the Westerly Patricia Hackett Prize, the Overland Judith Wright Poetry Prize, and grants from the Australia Council for the Arts (now Creative Australia) and Creative Victoria. Much gratitude to the always excellent team at Giramondo – especially Ivor Indyk, Aleesha Paz, Nick Tapper and Kate Prendergast. Heartfelt thanks also to: Alison Wong, for steadfast moral support and close-reading multiple variations of the manuscript; Leigh McKinnon at the Golden Dragon Museum in Bendigo for facilitating the lockdown reading group and for being such an amazing tour guide; Sophie Couchman and Paul MacGregor for so generously sharing knowledge and resources on Chinese Australian history; Demelza Wong for the superb illustrations; and my dearest family and friends for being my biggest champions. Deep gratitude and respect to the ancestors for having the fortitude and audacity to call Australia and Aotearoa home.

About the Author

Grace Yee lives in Melbourne, on Wurundjeri land. Her poetry has been widely published and anthologised in Australia and internationally, and has been awarded the Patricia Hackett Prize, the Peter Steele Poetry Award, and a Creative Fellowship at the State Library Victoria. She has taught in the creative writing programs at Deakin University, and at the University of Melbourne, where she completed a PhD on settler Chinese women's storytelling in Aotearoa New Zealand. Her debut collection *Chinese Fish* won the Victorian Prize for Literature, the Victorian Premier's Literary Award for Poetry, and the Mary and Peter Biggs Award for Poetry at the Ockham New Zealand Book Awards. graceyeepoet.com